Prayers
to help you through the week

Text compiled by Olivia Warburton
This edition copyright © 2003 Lion Publishing

Published by
Lion Publishing plc
Mayfield House, 256 Banbury Road,
Oxford OX2 7DH, England
www.lion-publishing.co.uk
ISBN 0 7459 4852 9

First edition 2003
10 9 8 7 6 5 4 3 2 1 0

A catalogue record for this book is available
from the British Library

Typeset in 12/15 Lapidary 333
Printed and bound in Finland

Prayers

to help you through the week

A LION BOOK

Before I even speak a word,
you know what I will say.

Psalm 139:4

Contents

Introduction

Prayers to Help You Through the Week aims to do just that. It's a book for everyone who wants to see prayer making a difference to their life each day. And it's a book that can be used flexibly in a range of situations, whether you're struggling to get out of bed on Monday morning, or in survival mode until the weekend comes round again; looking for a quiet moment in a busy day, or searching for words to express how you're feeling; happy or sad, or pondering the meaning of life.

An eclectic mix drawn from across the centuries and from different countries and traditions, from songs and speeches, from private writings and the Bible, the prayers are arranged in seven sections, one for each day of the week. This allows the reader to work through the book day by day, but each section also has a particular theme, so that the book can be used when you are feeling a certain way or needing to gain inspiration for a specific situation.

Monday's theme is the need to rely on God and develop a close relationship with him.

Tuesday's theme is 'today': committing the day ahead to God and asking for his involvement in all that happens.

Wednesday's theme is busyness and stress, and the need to find peace and rest amongst the pressures of daily life.

Thursday's theme is difficulty – trouble or suffering. These are prayers to call out to God when perhaps one's own words don't come easily.

Friday's theme is prayer for other people and for our relationship with them, whether they are friends or family or colleagues or neighbours with whom there is daily contact, or people in distant lands whom we may never meet.

Saturday's theme is journeying and pathways, seeking God's direction for the way ahead and his guidance for the future.

Sunday's theme is praise and worship, providing ways to express love to God and thank him for his love for us.

Monday

My spirit has become dry
because it forgets to feed on you.

St John of the Cross

Monday

O God, my guardian,
stay always with me.
In the morning,
in the evening,
by day or by night,
always be my helper.

Polish prayer

Lord, I am yours,
I was born for you;
what is your will for me?
Let me be rich or beggared,
exulting or lamenting,
comforted or lonely;
since I am yours,
yours only,
what is your will for me?

St Teresa of Avila

Lord of the loving heart,
May mine be loving too;
Lord of the gentle hands,
May mine be gentle too;
Lord of the willing feet,
May mine be willing too,
So I may grow more like thee
In all I say and do.

Anon

O great chief,
light a candle within my heart
that I may see what is therein
and sweep the rubbish
from your dwelling place.

African prayer

Monday

You have looked deep
into my heart, Lord,
and you know all about me.
You know when I am resting
or when I am working,
and from heaven
you discover my thoughts.

You notice everything I do
and everywhere I go.
Before I even speak a word,
you know what I will say,
and with your powerful arm
you protect me from every side.
I can't understand all this!
Such wonderful knowledge
is far above me.

Where could I go to escape
from your Spirit
or from your sight?
If I were to climb up
to the highest heavens,
you would be there.
If I were to dig down
to the world of the dead
you would also be there.

Suppose I had wings
like the dawning day
and flew across the ocean.
Even then your powerful arm
would guide and protect me.
Or suppose I said, 'I'll hide
in the dark until night comes
to cover me over.'

Monday

But you see in the dark
because daylight and dark
are all the same to you.

You are the one who put me together
inside my mother's body,
and I praise you
because of the wonderful way
you created me.
Everything you do is marvellous!
Of this I have no doubt.

Nothing about me
is hidden from you!
I was secretly woven together
deep in the earth below,
but with your own eyes
you saw my body being formed.
Even before I was born,

you had written in your book
everything I would do.

Your thoughts are far beyond
my understanding,
much more than
I could ever imagine.
I try to count your thoughts,
but they outnumber the grains
of sand on the beach.
And when I awake,
I will find you nearby.

Look deep into my heart, God,
and find out everything
I am thinking.
Don't let me follow evil ways,
but lead me in the way
that time has proved true.

Psalm 139:1–18, 23–24

Monday

Take my life and let it be
Consecrated, Lord, to thee:
Take my moments and my days,
Let them flow in ceaseless praise.

Take my hands and let them move
At the impulse of thy love:
Take my feet and let them be
Swift and beautiful for thee.

Take my voice and let me sing
Always, only, for my King:
Take my lips and let them be
Filled with messages from thee.

Take my silver and my gold,
Not a mite would I withhold:
Take my intellect and use
Every power as thou shalt choose.

Take my will and make it thine;
It shall be no longer mine:
Take my heart, it is thine own;
It shall be thy royal throne.

Take my love; my Lord, I pour
At thy feet its treasure store:
Take myself and I will be
Ever, only, all for thee.

Frances Ridley Havergal

Teach me, my God and King,
In all things thee to see,
And what I do in anything,
To do it as for thee.

George Herbert

Monday

Behold, Lord,

an empty vessel

that needs to be filled.

My Lord, fill it.

I am weak in the faith;

strengthen me.

I am cold in love;

warm me and make me fervent

that my love may go out to my neighbour.

I do not have a strong and firm faith;

at times I doubt

and am unable to trust you altogether.

O Lord, help me

and strengthen my faith

and trust in you.

Martin Luther

Breathe in me, Holy Spirit,

that I may think what is holy.

Move me, Holy Spirit,

that I may do what is holy.

Attract me, Holy Spirit,

that I may love what is holy.

Strengthen me, Holy Spirit,

that I may guard what is holy.

Guard me, Holy Spirit,

that I may keep what is holy.

St Augustine of Hippo

Lord, let the flame of your love

set on fire my whole heart.

May I wholly burn towards you,

wholly love you, set aflame by you.

St Augustine of Hippo

Monday

Create in me a pure heart, O God,
and renew a steadfast spirit within me.
Do not cast me from your presence
or take your Holy Spirit from me.

Psalm 51:10–11

Breathe on me, breath of God,
And fill my life anew;
That I may love as you love,
And do the works that you do.
Holy Spirit, breathe on me.

Breathe on me, breath of God,
Until my heart is pure;
Until my will is one with yours,
Let holiness and love endure.
Holy Spirit, breathe on me.

Edwin Hatch

Is there any forgiveness
For the things I've done?
Is there pardon for sinners?
I know that I'm one before you.

Would you take this heart of foulness,
Make it clean again?
Would you pour on me your mercy
As I confess my sin before you?

Point my feet in the way they should go.
Place your Holy Spirit in me.
Lead me in the ways everlasting –
I long to have a heart that's pure.
I need to have a heart that's pure before you.

O Lord, forgive me.
I need your mercy.

Randy Butler

Monday

Eternal Light,

shine into our hearts,

eternal Goodness,

deliver us from evil,

eternal Power,

be our support,

eternal Wisdom,

scatter the darkness of our ignorance,

eternal Pity,

have mercy upon us;

that with all our heart and mind

and soul and strength

we may seek your face

and be brought by your infinite mercy

to your holy presence;

through Jesus Christ our Lord.

Alcuin of York

Eternal and most glorious God,

suffer me not so to undervalue myself

as to give away my soul, thy soul,

thy dear and precious soul, for nothing;

and all the world is nothing,

if the soul be given for it.

Preserve therefore my soul, O Lord,

because it belongs to thee,

and preserve my body

because it belongs to my soul.

John Donne

Give us, O God, the needs the body feels,

Give us, God, the need-things of the soul;

Give us, O God, the balm which body heals,

Give us, God, the soul-balm which makes whole.

Celtic prayer

Monday

God give us rain

when we expect sun.

Give us music

when we expect trouble.

Give us tears

when we expect breakfast.

Give us dreams

when we expect a storm.

Give us a stray dog

when we expect congratulations.

God play with us,

turn us sideways and around.

Michael Leunig

God bless our contradictions,
those parts of us
which seem out of character.
Let us be boldly and gladly
out of character.
Let us be creatures
of paradox and variety:
creatures of contrast;
of light and shade:
creatures of faith.
God be our constant.
Let us step out of character
into the unknown,
to struggle and love
and do what we will.

Michael Leunig

Monday

Christ be with me,
Christ within me,
Christ behind me,
Christ before me,
Christ beside me,
Christ to win me,
Christ to comfort
and restore me.
Christ beneath me,
Christ above me,
Christ in quiet
and Christ in danger,
Christ in hearts of
all that love me,
Christ in mouth of
friend and stranger.

St Patrick of Ireland

I am only a spark;
Make me a fire.
I am only a string;
Make me a lyre.
I am only a drop;
Make me a fountain.
I am only an anthill;
Make me a mountain.
I am only a feather;
Make me a wing.
I am only a rag;
Make me a king!

Mexican prayer

Tuesday

Lord, let me not live
to be useless.

John Wesley

Tuesday

Come into my soul, Lord,
as the dawn breaks into the sky;
let your sun rise in my heart
at the coming of the day.

Anon

God, who hast folded back
the mantle of the night
to clothe us
in the golden glory of the day,
chase from our hearts
all gloomy thoughts
and make us glad
with the brightness of hope.

Traditional collect

Day by day,

dear Lord, of thee

three things I pray:

to see thee more clearly,

love thee more dearly,

follow thee more nearly,

day by day.

St Richard of Chichester

Holy, holy, holy, Lord God Almighty!

Early in the morning

our song shall rise to thee.

John B. Dykes and Reginald Heber

Let this day, O Lord,

add some knowledge or good deed

to yesterday.

Lancelot Andrewes

Tuesday

Dear Lord Jesus,
we shall have this day only once;
before it is gone,
help us to do all the good we can,
so that today is not a wasted day.

Stephen Grellet

God give me work
till my life shall end
and life
till my work is done.

On the grave of Winifred Holtby

The things, good Lord,
that I pray for,
give me the grace
to labour for.

Thomas More

Lord, you know the fears and anxieties

that fill our hearts at what today will bring.

Free us from panic and worry.

Anchor our thoughts and minds

in your great power and love.

Send us into this day

with your peace in our hearts

and sure confidence

in your fatherly care.

Through Jesus Christ our Lord.

Anon

Bless to me, O God,

the work of my hands.

Bless to me, O God,

the work of my mind.

Bless to me, O God,

the work of my heart.

Anon

Tuesday

Lord, help me today to realize
that you will be speaking to me
through the events of the day,
through people, through things,
and through all creation.
Give me ears, eyes and heart
to perceive you,
however veiled your presence may be.
Give me insight
to see through the exterior of things
to the interior truth.
Give me your spirit of discernment.
O Lord, you know how busy I must be this day.
If I forget you, do not forget me.

Jacob Astley

Father God,
please help me today.

Give me patience with my work
when there is so much to do
in so little time,
and I despair of finishing the job
or of doing it well.

Give me patience with other people
when there are difficult situations,
or when I simply do not feel able
to spend time building relationships.

Give me patience with life
when time passes
and dreams do not seem to come true.
Give me hope and trust in you.

Based on a prayer by William Barclay

Tuesday

Lord,

help me to live this day

quietly, easily.

Help me to lean upon

thy great strength

trustfully, restfully,

to wait

for the unfolding of thy will

patiently, serenely,

to meet others

peacefully, joyously,

to face tomorrow

confidently, courageously.

St Francis of Assisi

God to surround me,

God to encompass me;

God in my words,

God in my thought;

God in my waking,

God in my resting;

God in my hoping,

God in my doing;

God in my heart,

God in my soul;

God in my weakness,

God in my strength;

God in my life,

God in eternity;

God in my life,

God in eternity.

W. Mary Calvert

Tuesday

In every day that dawns,
I see the light of your splendour around me;
And everywhere I turn,
I know the gift of your favour upon me.
What can I do but give you glory, Lord?
Everything good has come from you.

I'm grateful for the air I breathe,
I'm so thankful for this life I live,
For the mercies that you pour on me,
And the blessings that meet every need,
And the grace that is changing me
From a hopeless case to a child that's free,
Free to give you praise,
For in everything I know you love me.

Kate Simmonds and Stuart Townend

Lord Jesus Christ,

fill us, we pray, with your light

that we may reflect your wondrous glory.

So fill us with your love

that we may count

nothing too small to do for you,

nothing too much to give,

and nothing too hard to bear.

St Ignatius Loyola

Here I am, Lord –

body, heart and soul.

Grant that with your love

I may be big enough

to reach the world

and small enough

to be at one with you.

Mother Teresa of Calcutta

Tuesday

Lord, I come to you,
Let my heart be changed, renewed,
Flowing from the grace
That I found in you.

And, Lord, I've come to know
The weaknesses I see in me
Will be stripped away
By the power of your love.

Hold me close,
Let your love surround me.
Bring me near,
Draw me to your side.
And as I wait,
I'll rise up like the eagle,
And I will soar with you,
Your Spirit leads me on
In the power of your love.

Lord, unveil my eyes,
Let me see you face to face,
The knowledge of your love
As you live in me.

Lord, renew my mind,
As your will unfolds in my life,
In living every day
By the power of your love.

Geoff Bullock

O Lord our God,
give us by your Holy Spirit
a willing heart and a ready hand
to use all your gifts to your praise and glory;
through Jesus Christ our Lord.

Thomas Cranmer

Tuesday

Lord of all hopefulness,
Lord of all joy,
Whose trust, ever childlike,
No cares could destroy,
Be there at our waking,
And give us, we pray,
Your bliss in our hearts, Lord,
At the break of the day.

Lord of all eagerness,
Lord of all faith,
Whose strong hands were skilled
At the plane and the lathe,
Be there at our labours
And give us, we pray,
Your strength in our hearts, Lord,
At the noon of the day.

Lord of all kindliness,
Lord of all grace,
Your hands swift to welcome,
Your arms to embrace,
Be there at our homing
And give us, we pray,
Your love in our hearts, Lord,
At the eve of the day.

Lord of all gentleness,
Lord of all calm,
Whose voice is contentment,
Whose presence is balm,
Be there at our sleeping
And give us, we pray,
Your peace in our hearts, Lord,
At the end of the day.

Jan Struther

Tuesday

O God, you have formed heaven and earth;
you have given me all the goods
that the earth bears!
Here is your part, my God.
Take it!

African prayer

We commend unto you, O Lord,
our souls and our bodies,
our minds and our thoughts,
our prayers and our hopes,
our health and our work,
our life and our death,
our parents and brothers and sisters,
our benefactors and friends,
our neighbours, our countrymen,
and all Christian folk,
this day and always.

Lancelot Andrewes

Our Father in heaven,

hallowed be your name,

your kingdom come;

your will be done,

on earth as in heaven.

Give us today our daily bread.

Forgive us our sins

as we forgive those who sin against us.

Lead us not into temptation

but deliver us from evil.

For the kingdom, the power, and the glory are yours,

now and for ever.

The Lord's prayer

Wednesday

O God,
make us children of quietness,
and heirs of peace.

St Clement of Alexandria

Wednesday

Lord, temper with tranquillity
Our manifold activity,
That we may do our work for thee
With very great simplicity.

Monastic prayer

O God, grant us the serenity
to accept what cannot be changed,
the courage to change what can be changed
and the wisdom to know the difference.

Reinhold Niebuhr

Even as the water falls on dry tea leaves
and brings out their flavour,
so may your Spirit fall on us and renew us
so that we may bring
refreshment and joy to others.

Sri Lankan prayer

In the rush and noise of life,
as you have intervals,
step within yourselves
and be still.
Wait upon God
and feel his good presence;
this will carry you
through your day's business.

William Penn

Good Jesus,
strength of the weary,
rest of the restless,
by the weariness and unrest
of your sacred cross,
come to me who am weary
that I may rest in you.

Edward Pusey

Wednesday

God help us to find our confession;
the truth within us which is hidden from our mind;
the beauty or the ugliness we see elsewhere
but never in ourselves;
the stowaway which has been smuggled
into the dark side of the heart,
which puts the heart off-balance and causes it pain,
which wearies and confuses us,
which tips us in false directions
and inclines us to destruction,
the load which is not carried squarely
because it is carried in ignorance.
God help us to find our confession.
Help us across the boundary of our understanding.
Lead us into the darkness
that we may find what lies concealed;

that we may confess it towards the light;

that we may carry our truth

in the centre of our heart;

that we may carry our cross wisely

and bring harmony into our life and our world.

Michael Leunig

Father in heaven,

when the thought of you

wakes in our hearts,

let it not wake like a frightened bird

that flies about in dismay,

but like a child waking from its sleep

with a heavenly smile.

Anon

Wednesday

In the stillness,
you are there.

In the silence,
you are there.

When the talking stops,
I can pray.

When the talking stops,
I can hear your voice.

Anon

All is silent.
In the still and soundless air,
I fervently bow
to my almighty God.

Hsieh Ping-hsin, China

O make my heart so still, so still,

When I am deep in prayer,

That I might hear the white mist-wreaths

Losing themselves in air!

Utsonomya San, Japan

God rest us.

Rest that part of us

which is tired.

Awaken that part of us

which is asleep.

God awaken us

and awake within us.

Anon

Wednesday

May the Light of lights come
to my dark heart from thy place;
may the Spirit's wisdom come
to my heart's tablet from my Saviour.
Be the peace of the Spirit mine this night,
be the peace of the Son mine this night,
the peace of all peace be mine this night,
each morning and evening of my life.

Celtic prayer

Drop thy still dews of quietness,
Till all our strivings cease;
Take from our souls the strain and stress,
And let our ordered lives confess
The beauty of thy peace.

John Greenleaf Whittier

Deep peace of the running waves to you,

deep peace of the flowing air to you,

deep peace of the quiet earth to you,

deep peace of the shining stars to you,

deep peace of the shades of night to you,

moon and stars always giving light to you,

deep peace of Christ, the Son of Peace, to you.

Celtic prayer

Send your peace into my heart, O Lord,

that I may be contented

with your mercies of this day

and confident of your protection for this night;

and having forgiven others,

even as you forgive me,

may I go to my rest in peaceful trust

through Jesus Christ, our Lord.

St Francis of Assisi

Wednesday

I look to the hills!
Where will I find help?
It will come from the Lord,
who created the heavens
and the earth.

The Lord is your protector,
and he won't go to sleep
or let you stumble.
The protector of Israel doesn't doze
or ever get drowsy.

The Lord is your protector,
there at your right side
to shade you from the sun.
You won't be harmed
by the sun during the day
or by the moon at night.

The Lord will protect you

and keep you safe from all dangers.

The Lord will protect you

now and always, wherever you go.

Psalm 121

God be in my head,

and in my understanding;

God be in my eyes,

and in my looking;

God be in my mouth,

and in my speaking;

God be in my heart,

and in my thinking;

God be at my end

and at my departing.

Sarum Primer

Thursday

Dear God, be good to me;
the sea is so large,
and my boat is so small.

Breton fisherman's prayer

Thursday

From a sea of troubles
I call out to you, Lord.
Won't you please listen
as I beg for mercy?

If you kept record of our sins,
no one could last long.
But you forgive us,
and so we will worship you.

With all my heart,
I am waiting, Lord, for you!
I trust your promises.
I wait for you more eagerly
than a soldier on guard duty
waits for the dawn.
Yes, I wait more eagerly
than a soldier on guard duty
waits for the dawn.

Psalm 130:1–6

Lord, I am tearing
the heart of my soul in two.
I need you to come
and lie there yourself
in the wounds of my soul.

Mechtild of Magdeburg

Abide with me;
Fast falls the eventide;
The darkness deepens;
Lord, with me abide;

When other helpers fail,
And other comforts flee,
Help of the helpless,
O abide with me.

Henry Francis Lyte

Thursday

O Lord, the help of the helpless,

the hope of the hopeless,

the saviour of the storm-tossed,

the harbour of voyagers,

the physician of the sick;

we pray to you.

O Lord, you know each of us and our petitions;

you know each house and its needs;

receive us all into your kingdom;

make us children of light,

and bestow your peace and love upon us.

St Basil of Caesarea

O God, our help in ages past,

Our hope for years to come,

Be thou our guard while troubles last,

And our eternal home.

Isaac Watts

Lord, you carry me over the troublesome waters.

My arms are raised.

As you lead me to salvation,

My arms are raised.

For you reached out to me when I needed you most.

My arms are raised.

My eyes are closed, I feel your hand.

My arms are raised.

You lived and died for me.

My arms are raised.

I kneel down before you and give thanks.

My arms are raised.

Holding up the cross for ever and ever,

My arms are raised.

Angel Gardner

Thursday

Lord, make possible for me by grace
what is impossible to me by nature.
You know that I am not able to endure very much,
and that I am downcast by the slightest difficulty.
Grant that for your sake
I may come to love and desire any hardship
that puts me to the test,
for salvation is brought to my soul
when I undergo suffering and trouble for you.

Thomas à Kempis

O Father God,
I cannot fight this darkness
by beating it with my hands.
Help me to take the light of Christ
right into it.

African prayer

My strength fails;

I feel only weakness, irritation and depression.

I am tempted to complain and to despair.

What has become of the courage I was so proud of

and that gave me so much self-confidence?

In addition to my pain,

I have to bear the shame of my fretful feebleness.

Lord, destroy my pride;

leave it no resource.

How happy I shall be

if you can teach me by these terrible trials

that I am nothing,

that I can do nothing

and that you are all!

François Fenelon

Thursday

Hear my voice when I call, O Lord;
be merciful to me and answer me.
My heart says of you, 'Seek his face!'
Your face, Lord, I will seek.
Do not hide your face from me,
do not turn your servant away in anger;
you have been my helper.
Do not reject me or forsake me.

Psalm 27:7–9

As the tropical sun
gives forth its light,
so let the rays
from your face, O God,
enter every nook
of my being,
and drive away
all the dreariness within.

Filipino prayer

Ah Lord, my prayers are dead,

my affections are dead

and my heart is dead;

but you are a living God

and I bear myself upon you.

William Bridge

You who guided Noah

over the flood waves:

hear us.

You who with your word

recalled Jonah from the deep:

deliver us.

You who stretched forth your hand

to Peter as he sank:

help us, O Christ.

Son of God, who did marvellous things of old:

be favourable in our day also.

Celtic prayer

Thursday

Father in heaven,
you speak to us in many ways.
Even when you are silent,
you still speak to us,
in order to examine us,
to try us,
and so that the hour of our understanding
may be more profound.
Oh, in the time of silence,
when I remain alone and abandoned
because I do not hear your voice,
it seems as if the separation
must last for ever.
Father in heaven!
It is only a moment of silence
in the intimacy of a conversation.

Bless then this silence,

and let me not forget

that you are silent through love,

and that you speak through love,

so that in your silence

and in your word

you are still the same Father,

and that you guide and instruct

even by your silence.

Søren Kierkegaard

I believe in the sun

even when it is not shining.

I believe in love

even when I don't feel it.

I believe in God

even when he is silent.

German prayer

Thursday

You, Lord, are the light
that keeps me safe.
I am not afraid of anyone.
You protect me,
and I have no fears.

I ask only one thing, Lord:
let me live in your house
every day of my life
to see how wonderful you are
and to pray in your temple.

In times of trouble,
you will protect me.
You will hide me in your tent
and keep me safe
on top of a mighty rock.

Psalm 27:1, 4–5

Faithful one, so unchanging,

Ageless one, you're my rock of peace.

Lord of all, I depend on you.

I call out to you again and again.

You are my rock in times of trouble.

You lift me up when I fall down.

All through the storm your love is the anchor.

My hope is in you alone.

Brian Doerksen

As the rain hides the stars,

as the autumn mist hides the hills,

as the clouds veil the blue of the sky,

so the dark happenings of my lot

hide the shining of your face from me.

Yet, if I may hold your hand in the darkness,

it is enough, since I know that,

though I may stumble in my going,

you do not fall.

Celtic prayer, translated by Alistair MacLean

Friday

Pour forth, O Christ,
your love upon this land today.

Anon

Friday

May I be no man's enemy,
and may I be the friend
of that which is eternal and abides.
May I never quarrel with those nearest me;
and if I do, may I never devise evil against any man;
if any devise evil against me,
may I escape uninjured
and without the need of hurting him.
May I love, seek and attain
only that which is good.
May I wish for all men's happiness and envy none.
May I never rejoice in the ill-fortune
of one who has wronged me.
When I have done or said what is wrong,
may I never wait for the rebuke of others,
but always rebuke myself until I make amends.
May I win no victory
that harms either me or my opponent.

May I reconcile friends

who are wroth with one another.

May I, to the extent of my power,

give all needful help to my friends

and to all who are in want.

May I never fail a friend in danger.

When visiting those in grief,

may I be able by gentle and healing words

to soften their pain.

May I respect myself.

May I accustom myself to be gentle,

and never be angry with people

because of circumstances.

May I never discuss who is wicked

and what wicked things he has done,

but know good men and follow in their footsteps.

Eusebius

Friday

O God of love,

we ask you to give us love;

love in our thinking,

love in our speaking,

love in our doing,

and love in the hidden places of our souls;

love of those

with whom we find it hard to bear,

and love of those

who find it hard to bear with us;

love of those

with whom we work,

and love of those

with whom we take our ease;

that so at length we may be worthy

to dwell with you,

who are eternal love.

William Temple

Grant me grace, Lord,

to be strong and wise in all things.

Give me a generous love.

Fill me with the spirit of intelligence and wisdom.

Let me always be mindful of others.

O perfect and eternal Light,

enlighten me.

Alcuin of York

God our Father, creator of the world,

please help us to love one another.

Make nations friendly with other nations;

make all of us love one another

like brothers and sisters.

Help us to do our part to bring

peace in the world

and happiness to all people.

Japanese prayer

Friday

Grant unto us your servants
to our God – a heart of flame;
to our fellow men – a heart of love;
to ourselves – a heart of steel.

St Augustine of Hippo

Almighty God and most merciful Father,
who has given us a new commandment
that we should love one another,
give us also grace that we may fulfil it.
Make us gentle, courteous and forbearing.
Direct our lives so that we may look
to the good of the other in word and deed.
And hallow all our friendships
by the blessing of your Spirit,
for his sake who loved us and gave himself for us,
Jesus Christ our Lord.

Brooke Foss Westcott

Lord, make me an instrument of your peace.

Where there is hatred, let me sow love;

where there is injury, pardon;

where there is discord, union;

where there is doubt, faith;

where there is despair, hope;

where there is darkness, light;

where there is sadness, joy.

O Divine Master,

grant that I may not so much seek

to be consoled as to console;

to be understood as to understand;

to be loved as to love;

for it is in giving that we receive,

it is in pardoning that we are pardoned,

and it is in dying that we are born to eternal life.

Attributed to St Francis of Assisi

Friday

Lord, you taught us
that all who come our way are our neighbours.
But hear our prayer for those with whom
we come in daily contact because they live close to us.
Help us to be good neighbours to them.
Give us the grace to overlook petty annoyances
and to build on all that is positive in our relationship,
that we may love them as we love ourselves,
with genuine forbearance and kindness.
For Jesus' sake.

Anon

O Lord, help us to be
masters of ourselves
that we may be
the servants of others.

Alexander Henry Paterson

O God,

who gives to your children liberally,

preserve us from all envy

at the good of our neighbour

and from every form of jealousy.

Teach us to rejoice in what others have

and we have not,

to delight in what they achieve

and we cannot accomplish,

to be glad in all that they enjoy

and we do not partake of;

and so fill us daily

more completely with love,

through our Saviour Jesus Christ.

William Knight

Friday

Lord, open our eyes,

that we may see you in our brothers and sisters;

Lord, open our ears,

that we may hear the cries from the hungry,

the frightened, the oppressed.

Lord, open our hands,

that we may reach out to all who are in need;

Lord, open our hearts,

that we may love each other as you love us.

Canadian prayer

We pray, mighty God, for those who struggle,

that their life's flickering flame may not be snuffed out.

We pray for the poor and deprived,

for those exploited by the powerful and greedy,

and for a more human sharing of the plenty

you have given your world.

Indian prayer

O God,

the refuge of the poor,

the strength of those who toil

and the comforter of all who sorrow,

we commend to your mercy

the unfortunate and needy

in whatever land they may be.

You alone know the number and extent

of their sufferings and trials.

Look down, Father of mercies,

at those unhappy families

suffering from war and slaughter,

from hunger and disease

and other severe trials.

Spare them, O Lord,

for it is truly a time for mercy.

Peter Canisius

Friday

O God our Father,

in the name of him

who gave bread to the hungry

we remember all

who through our human ignorance,

selfishness and sin

are condemned to live in want;

and we pray that all endeavours

for the overcoming

of world poverty and hunger

may be so prospered

that there may be found

food sufficient for all;

through Jesus Christ our Lord.

Anon

O God, help us not to despise or oppose

what we do not understand.

William Penn

Watch, dear Lord,

with those who wake,

or watch, or weep tonight,

and give your angels

charge over those who sleep;

tend your sick ones,

O Lord Christ,

rest your weary ones,

bless your dying ones,

soothe your suffering ones,

pity your afflicted ones,

shield your joyous ones,

and all for your love's sake.

St Augustine of Hippo

Friday

Father, take all the broken bits of our lives:
our broken promises;
our broken friendships;
our differences of opinion;
our different backgrounds,
and shapes and sizes;
and arrange them together,
fitting them into each other
to make something beautiful
like an artist makes
a stained glass window.
Make a design,
your design,
even when all we can see
are the broken bits.

Anon

Liberating one,

free us from all bondage

so that our faith in you

will make us free to create with courage

a new world – new societies.

Sri Lankan prayer

Father of all mankind,

make the roof of my house

wide enough for all opinions,

oil the door of my house

so it opens easily to friend and stranger,

and set such a table in my house

that my whole family may speak

kindly and freely around it.

Hawaian prayer

Friday

Now to the Father
who created each creature,
now to the Son
who paid ransom for his people,
now to the Holy Spirit,
comforter of might:
shield and deliver us
from every wound;
be about the beginning and end of our race,
be giving us to sing in glory,
in peace, in rest, in reconciliation,
where no tear shall be shed,
where death comes no more,
where no tear shall be shed,
where death comes no more.

Carmina Gadelica

To you, O Son of God, Lord Jesus Christ,

as you pray to the eternal Father,

we pray, make us one in him.

Lighten our personal distress

and that of our society.

Receive us into the fellowship

of those who believe.

Turn our hearts, O Christ,

to everlasting truth and healing harmony.

Philip Melanchthon

May the road rise up to meet you,

may the wind be always at your back,

may the sun shine upon your face,

the rains fall soft upon your fields

and, until we meet again,

may God hold you in the palm of his hand.

Celtic prayer

Saturday

Alone with none but thee, my God,

I journey on my way.

St Columba of Iona

Saturday

Father, I am seeking:
I am hesitant and uncertain,
but will you, O God,
watch over each step of mine
and guide me.

St Augustine of Hippo

Show me your ways, O Lord,
teach me your paths;
guide me in your truth
and teach me,
for you are God my Saviour,
and my hope is in you
all day long.

Psalm 25:4–5

God before me,

God behind me,

God above me,

God below me;

I on the path of God,

God upon my track.

Who is there on land?

Who is there on wave?

Who is there on billow?

Who is there by door post?

Who is there along with us?

God and Lord.

I am here abroad,

I am here in need,

I am here in pain,

I am here in straits,

I am here alone,

O God, aid me.

Celtic prayer

Saturday

O Lord, this is our desire:
to walk along the path of life
that you have appointed us,
in steadfastness of faith,
in lowliness of heart,
in gentleness of love.
Let not the cares or duties of this life
press on us too heavily;
but lighten our burdens,
that we may follow your way
in quietness,
filled with thankfulness
for your mercy;
through Jesus Christ our Lord.

Maria Hare

O Lord, whose way is perfect:

help us, we pray,

always to trust in your goodness;

that walking with you in faith,

and following you in all simplicity,

we may possess quiet and contented minds,

and cast all our care on you,

because you care for us;

for the sake of Jesus Christ our Lord.

Christina Rossetti

Alone with none but thee, my God,

I journey on my way.

What need I fear, when thou art near,

O King of night and day?

More safe am I within thy hand

Than if a host did round me stand.

St Columba of Iona

Saturday

Lord God,

thank you for loving us

even when we turn away from you.

We are grateful

for your constant care and concern.

Though we feel unworthy

of your great love,

we thank you that

through our weaknesses

you give us strength;

and in our wanderings

you show us the way.

Anon

Let us make our way together, Lord;

wherever you go I must go:

and through whatever you pass,

there too I will pass.

St Teresa of Avila

Dear Lord, I may not see
the sun and moon lose their light.
I may not witness rivers turn red,
or stars fall from the sky.
Yet there are times
when my world becomes unhinged
and the foundations of what I believe
crack and dissolve.
Give me the grace to believe
that your power is at work
in the turmoil of my life.
Lead me to remember
that your power is greater than all evil,
and though the world may rock
and sometimes break,
it will in time be transformed
by your love.

Anon

Saturday

You, Lord, are my shepherd.
I will never be in need.
You let me rest in fields of green grass.
You lead me to streams
of peaceful water,
and you refresh my life.

You are true to your name,
and you lead me
along the right paths.
I may walk through valleys
as dark as death,
but I won't be afraid.
You are with me,
and your shepherd's rod
makes me feel safe.

You treat me to a feast,
while my enemies watch.

You honour me as your guest,

and you fill my cup until it overflows.

Your kindness and love

will always be with me

each day of my life,

and I will live for ever

in your house, Lord.

Psalm 23

My dearest Lord,

be thou a bright flame before me,

be thou a guiding star above me,

be thou a smooth path beneath me,

be thou a kindly shepherd behind me,

today and for evermore.

St Columba of Iona

Saturday

Dear Lord,
it's so difficult to know
what decisions to make
for the future.
I cannot see the path ahead
and I do not know
what the future will bring.
Only you know.

Please help me
to want only
what you want.
I know that
if this is my desire,
you will guide me,
even if it doesn't always
feel that way.

Even when I seem to be
lost in a dark valley,
I will not be afraid,
for you will never leave me
to make the journey alone.

Anon

Whoever truly loves you, good Lord,
walks in safety down a royal road,
far from the dangerous abyss;
and if he so much as stumbles,
you, O Lord, stretch out your hand.
Not one fall, or many,
will cause you to abandon him if he loves you
and does not love the things of this world,
because he walks in the vale of humility.

St Teresa of Avila

Saturday

Lead, kindly light,
Amid the encircling gloom,
Lead thou me on;
The night is dark,
And I am far from home;
Lead thou me on.
Keep thou my feet;
I do not ask to see
The distant scene;
One step enough for me.

John Henry Newman

Thy way, not mine, O Lord,
However dark it be;
Lead me by thine own hand,
Choose out the path for me.

Horatio Bonar

Move our hearts

with the calm, smooth flow of your grace.

Let the river of your love

run through our souls.

May my soul be carried

by the current of your love,

towards the wide, infinite ocean of heaven.

Gilbert of Hoyland

Lead us from death to life,

from falsehood to truth.

Lead us from despair to hope,

from fear to trust.

Lead us from hate to love,

from war to peace.

Let peace fill our hearts,

our world, our universe.

Anon

Sunday

Be thou my vision,
O Lord of my heart.

Eighth-century prayer

Sunday

Here I am once again,
I pour out my heart
For I know that you hear every cry;
You are listening,
No matter what state my heart is in.

You are faithful to answer
With words that are true
And a hope that is real.
As I feel your touch,
You bring a freedom
To all that's within.

In the safety of this place,
I'm longing to pour out my heart,
To say that I love you,
Pour out my heart,
To say that I need you.

Pour out my heart,
To say that I'm thankful,
Pour out my heart,
To say that you're wonderful.

Craig Musseau

Lord, you have my heart,
And I will search for yours;
Jesus, take my life and lead me on.

Lord, you have my heart,
And I will search for yours;
Let me be to you a sacrifice.

And I will praise you, Lord,
And I will sing of love come down;
And as you show your face,
We'll see your glory here.

Martin Smith

Sunday

You are my God.
I worship you.
In my heart, I long for you,
as I would long for a stream
in a scorching desert.

I have seen your power
and your glory
in the place of worship.
Your love means more than life to me,
and I praise you.
As long as I live,
I will pray to you.
I will sing joyful praises
and be filled with excitement
like a guest at a banquet.

I think about you before I go to sleep,
and my thoughts turn to you
during the night.

You have helped me,

and I sing happy songs

in the shadow of your wings.

I stay close to you,

and your powerful arm supports me.

Psalm 63:1–8

Praise God,

from whom all blessings flow,

praise him,

all creatures here below,

praise him above,

ye heavenly host,

praise Father, Son

and Holy Ghost.

Traditional prayer

Sunday

O praise God in his holy place,
praise him in the sky our tent,
praise him in the earth our mother;
praise him for his mighty works,
praise him for his marvellous power.
Praise him with the beating of great drums,
praise him with the horn and rattle;
praise him in the rhythm of the dance,
praise him in the clapping of the hands;
praise him in the stamping of the feet,
praise him in the singing of the chant.
Praise him with the rushing of great rivers,
praise him with the music of the wind;
praise him with the swaying of tall trees,
praise him with the singing of the sea.
Praise him, the one on whom we lean and do not fall;
let everything that has breath praise the Lord.

African prayer

As the hand is made for holding

and the eye for seeing,

you have fashioned me,

O Lord, for joy.

Share with me the vision

to find that joy everywhere:

in the wild violet's beauty,

in the lark's melody,

in the face of a steadfast man,

in a child's smile,

in a mother's love,

in the purity of Jesus.

Celtic prayer

There is no place where God is not;

wherever I go, there God is.

Now and always he upholds me with his power

and keeps me safe in his love.

Anon

Sunday

I believe,

O Lord and God of the peoples,

that you are

the creator of the high heavens,

that you are

the creator of the skies above,

that you are

the creator of the oceans below.

Carmina Gadelica

O God, we thank you for this earth,

our home;

for the wide sky and the blessed sun,

for the salt sea and the running water,

for the everlasting hills

and the never-resting winds,

for the trees

and the common grass underfoot.

We thank you for our senses
by which we hear the songs of birds,
and see the splendour of the summer fields,
and taste of the autumn fruits,
and rejoice in the feel of the snow
and smell the breath of the spring.

Grant us a heart
wide open to all this beauty;
and save our souls from being so blind
that we pass unseeing
when even the common thorn bush
is aflame with your glory,
O God our creator,
who lives and reigns for ever and ever.

Walter Rauschenbusch

Sunday

We celebrate the birth of Jesus:
for God has come among us.

We celebrate the birth of Jesus:
for heaven has come to earth.

We celebrate the birth of Jesus:
and let love grow between us.

We celebrate the birth of Jesus:
and live as God's children on earth.

Blessed be the name of Jesus,
who died to save us.

Blessed be Jesus,
who had compassion on us.

Blessed be Jesus,
who suffered loneliness, rejection and pain,
for our sakes.

Blessed be Jesus,

through whose cross I am forgiven.

Lord Jesus, deepen my understanding

of your suffering and death.

Kenyan prayer

I know a place, a wonderful place,

Where accused and condemned

Find mercy and grace.

Where the wrongs we have done,

And the wrongs done to us,

Were nailed there with you,

There on the cross.

At the cross you died for our sin.

At the cross you gave us life again.

Randy and Terry Butler

Sunday

I will worship
With all of my heart.
I will praise you
With all of my strength.

I will seek you
All of my days.
I will follow
All of your ways.

I will give you all my worship,
I will give you all my praise.
You alone I long to worship,
You alone are worthy of my praise.

I will bow down,
Hail you as king,
I will serve you,
Give you everything.

I will lift up
My eyes to your throne,
I will trust you,
I will trust you alone.

I will give you all my worship,
I will give you all my praise.
You alone I long to worship,
You alone are worthy of my praise.

David Ruis

O Christ, our Morning Star,
Splendour of Light Eternal,
shining with the glory of the rainbow,
come and waken us
from the greyness of our apathy
and renew in us your gift of hope.

The Venerable Bede

Sunday

Lord, you have always given
bread for the coming day;
and though I am poor,
today I believe.

Lord, you have always given
strength for the coming day;
and though I am weak,
today I believe.

Lord, you have always given
peace for the coming day;
and though of anxious heart,
today I believe.

Lord, you have always kept
me safe in trials;
and now, tried as I am,
today I believe.

Lord, you have always marked
the road for the coming day;
and though it may be hidden,
today I believe.

Lord, you have always lightened
this darkness of mine;
and though the night is here,
today I believe.

Lord, you have always spoken
when time was ripe;
and though you be silent now,
today I believe.

From the Northumbria Community

Sunday

Be thou my vision,
O Lord of my heart;
Be all else but naught to me,
Save that thou art;
Be thou my best thought
In the day and the night;
Both waking and sleeping,
Thy presence my light.

Be thou my wisdom,
Be thou my true word;
Be thou ever with me,
And I with thee, Lord;
Be thou my great Father,
And I thy true son;
Be thou in me dwelling,
And I with thee one.

Be thou my breastplate,
My sword for the fight;
Be thou my whole armour,
Be thou my true might;
Be thou my soul's shelter,
Be thou my strong tower;
O raise thou me heavenward,
Great Power of my power.

Riches I heed not,
Nor man's empty praise;
Be thou mine inheritance
Now and always;
Be thou and thou only
The first in my heart;
O Sovereign of heaven,
My treasure thou art.

Sunday

High King of heaven,

Thou heaven's bright Sun,

O grant me its joys

After victory is won;

Great Heart of my own heart,

Whatever befall,

Still be thou my vision,

O Ruler of all.

Eighth-century prayer, translated by Mary Byrne and Eleanor Hull

First line index

Author index

Acknowledgments

Every effort has been made to trace and contact copyright owners for material used in this book. We apologize for any inadvertent omissions or errors, and would ask those concerned to contact us so that full acknowledgment can be made in the future.

Pages 12, 56, 60, 70, 98, 108: Scripture quotations taken from the Contemporary English Version published by The Bible Societies/HarperCollins Publishers, copyright © 1991, 1992, 1995 American Bible Society.

Pages 20, 66, 92: Scripture quotations taken from the *Holy Bible, New International Version*, copyright © 1973, 1978, 1984 International Bible Society. Used by permission of Zondervan and Hodder & Stoughton Limited. All rights reserved. The 'NIV' and 'New International Version' trademarks are registered in the United States Patent and Trademark Office by International Bible Society. Use of either trademark requires the permission of International Bible Society. UK trademark number 1448790.

Pages 21, 71, 106, 115, 116: 'Before you' by Randy Butler; 'Faithful one' by Brian Doerksen; 'Pour out my heart' by Craig Musseau; 'I know a place' by Randy and Terry Butler; 'I will worship' by David Ruis, used with permission of Vineyard Songs (UK/Eire).

Page 24: copyright © 1990 and 1997 Michael Leunig, taken from *A Common Prayer* (Lion Publishing, 1997).

Pages 25, 50: copyright © 1991 Michael Leunig, taken from *The Prayer Tree* (Lion Publishing, 1997).

Page 38: 'In every day that dawns' by Kate Simmonds and Stuart Townend. Copyright © 2001 Thankyou Music. Adm. by worshiptogether.com songs excl. UK and Europe, adm. by Kingsway Music. tym@kingsway.co.uk. Used by permission.

Page 40: 'The power of your love' by Geoff Bullock. Copyright © 1992 Word Music Inc./Maranatha! Music, administered by CopyCare, P.O. Box 77, Hailsham BN27 3EF. music@copycare.com. Used by permission.

Page 107: 'Lord, you have my heart' by Martin Smith. Copyright © 1992 Thankyou Music. Adm. by worshiptogether.com songs excl. UK and Europe, adm. by Kingsway Music. tym@kingsway.co.uk. Used by permission.